I Can Make

COSTUMES

written and photographed by

Mary Wallace

Owl

Owl Books

I Can Make Costumes

Owl Books are published by Greey de Pencier Books Inc.,
179 John Street, Suite 500, Toronto, Ontario M5T 3G5

Owl and the Owl colophon are trademarks of Owl Communications.
Greey de Pencier Books Inc. is a licensed user of trademarks of Owl Communications.

Distributed in the United States by Firefly Books (U.S.) Inc.,
230 Fifth Avenue, Suite 1607, New York, NY 10001.

This book was published with the generous support of the Canada Council,
the Ontario Arts Council and the Ontario Publishing Centre.

Canadian Cataloguing in Publication Data

Wallace, Mary, 1950–
I can make costumes

ISBN 1-895688-46-9 (bound) ISBN 1-895688-47-7 (pbk.)

1. Costume – Juvenile literature. 2. Handicraft –
Juvenile literature. I. Title.

TT633.W34 1996   j646.4'78   C95-932253-1

Design & Art Direction: Julia Naimska

Costumes on the front cover, counterclockwise from upper left:
hat and wand from Magic Maker; Grecian robe from Toga Party; flowered hat from Just for Fun;
Fit for Royalty; Face Paint Fun; and Paper Bag Vest

The crafts in this book have been tested and are safe when conducted as instructed.
The author and publisher accept no responsibility for any damage caused or sustained
by the use or misuse of ideas or material featured in the crafts in *I Can Make Costumes*.

Other books by Mary Wallace
I Can Make Toys
I Can Make Puppets
I Can Make Gifts
I Can Make Games
I Can Make Nature Crafts
How to Make Great Stuff to Wear
How to Make Great Stuff for Your Room

Printed in Hong Kong

A   B   C   D   E   F

CONTENTS

LET'S MAKE COSTUMES

You can make and wear all the costumes in this book. It's easy. It's fun. These two pages show the things used to make the costumes in this book, but you can use other things if you like. You'll find most of what you need around the house — get permission to use what you find.

- safety pins
- rope
- crayons
- tempera paint
- aluminum foil
- Bristol board
- polyester stuffing
- stocking
- sweat suit
- cardboard box

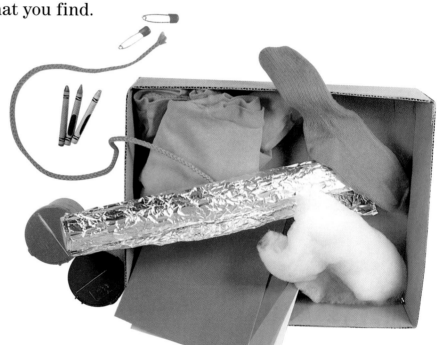

- pencil
- twist tie
- food coloring
- socks
- rubber band
- T-shirt
- markers
- tracing paper
- pillow
- paper bag

- metal paper fasteners
- corrugated cardboard
- colored tape
- hole punch
- plastic bags
- straws
- bath towel
- bowl
- cornstarch
- self-adhesive vinyl

- spoon
- shortening
- paintbrush
- yarn
- ice-cube tray
- paint stir stick
- masking tape
- colored paper
- paper tube
- acrylic paint

- fabric
- stretch pants
- newspaper
- white glue
- tape
- stapler
- scissors
- chalk
- ribbon

Hint: When stapling rings to fit around head, cover the inside surface with tape to keep staples from poking or catching.

JUST FOR FUN

If it was just for fun, think of who you could become . . .
Look around your house to find some things you could use to change the way
you look. Even the smallest changes in the way you look can make you feel like
a different person. So use your imagination and have fun dressing up!

Find some buttons, yarn, twist ties
and a safety pin and make a necklace,
a ring and a brooch.

Wrap up a ponytail and push in some straws.
Blow up balloons and fasten to straws with
twist ties.

An old hat becomes special with colorful flowers made from plastic bags.

Polyester stuffing glued on an old T-shirt looks like fur trim.

Film canisters snapped on fabric make bumps on a space glove or dinosaur scales down the back of a T-shirt.

put the lid inside and snap on over the fabric

Look through the book to get some other ideas!

7

SUPERHEROES

- large piece of knit fabric
- chalk
- scissors
- Bristol board
- colored tape
- stapler
- *decorate as you like*

CAPE

1 draw outline of cape with chalk

knit fabric

add lines for ties as shown

2 cut along chalk lines

trim bottom edge

MASK

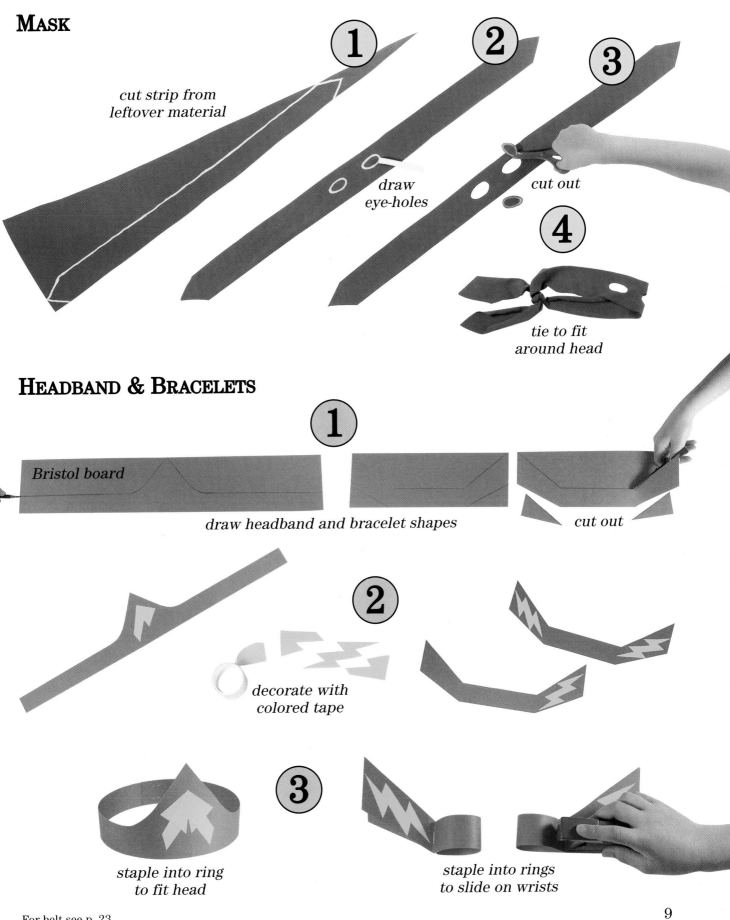

cut strip from
leftover material

1

2

draw
eye-holes

3

cut out

4

tie to fit
around head

HEADBAND & BRACELETS

1

Bristol board

draw headband and bracelet shapes

cut out

2

decorate with
colored tape

3

staple into ring
to fit head

staple into rings
to slide on wrists

For belt see p. 23.

When stapling ring, see p. 5.

PAPER BAG VEST

- large brown paper bag
- crayons
- scissors
- *decorate as you like*

1 *crinkle paper bag and smooth it out*

repeat until bag is soft

2 *draw and cut out arm and neck circles*

draw and cut front opening

trim bottom

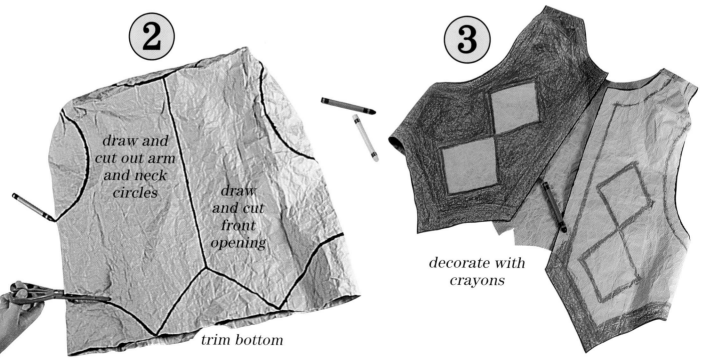

3 *decorate with crayons*

ORANGE SMILE

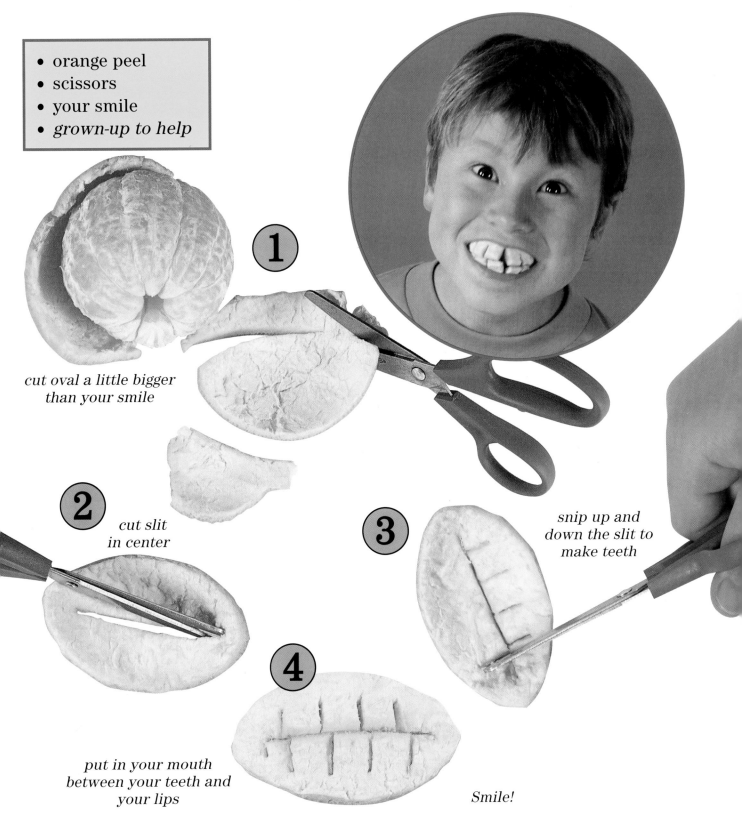

- orange peel
- scissors
- your smile
- *grown-up to help*

1

cut oval a little bigger
than your smile

2 cut slit
in center

3 snip up and
down the slit to
make teeth

4

put in your mouth
between your teeth and
your lips

Smile!

STAR EXPLORER

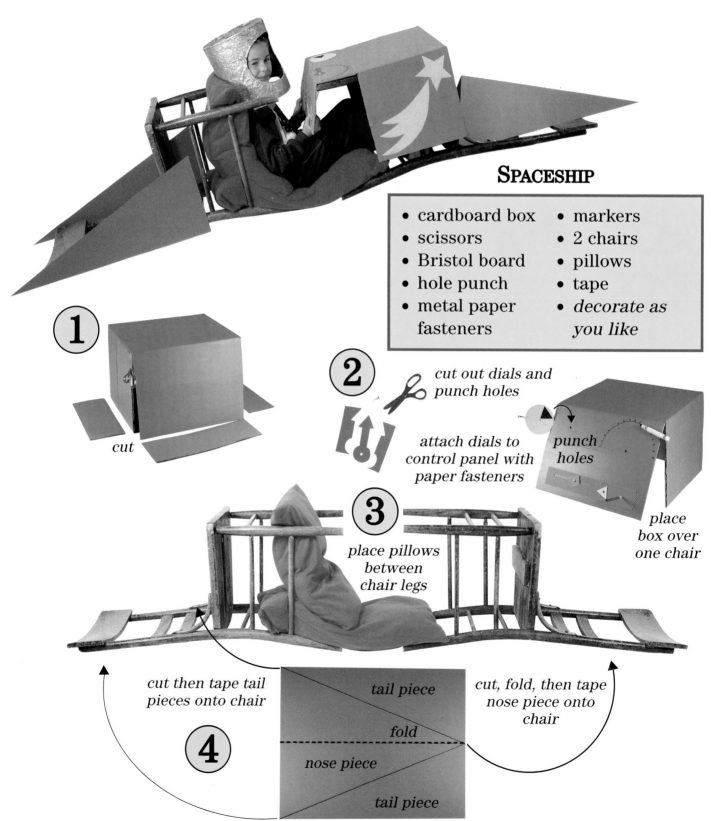

SPACESHIP

- cardboard box
- scissors
- Bristol board
- hole punch
- metal paper fasteners
- markers
- 2 chairs
- pillows
- tape
- *decorate as you like*

1 cut

2 cut out dials and punch holes

attach dials to control panel with paper fasteners

punch holes

place box over one chair

3 place pillows between chair legs

4 cut then tape tail pieces onto chair

tail piece

fold

nose piece

tail piece

cut, fold, then tape nose piece onto chair

SPACE HELMET

- container to fit over your head
- scissors
- aluminum foil
- tape
- *grown-up to help*

1 cut holes for shoulders

cut viewing hole

2 cover with aluminum foil

3 poke foil through holes and fold edges in

secure edges with tape

SPACE ALIEN

- Bristol board
- scissors
- stapler
- tape

1 cut 3 strips of Bristol board

2 staple short strips as shown

cut pieces from Bristol board and staple or tape on

staple long strip into ring to fit head

decorate as you like

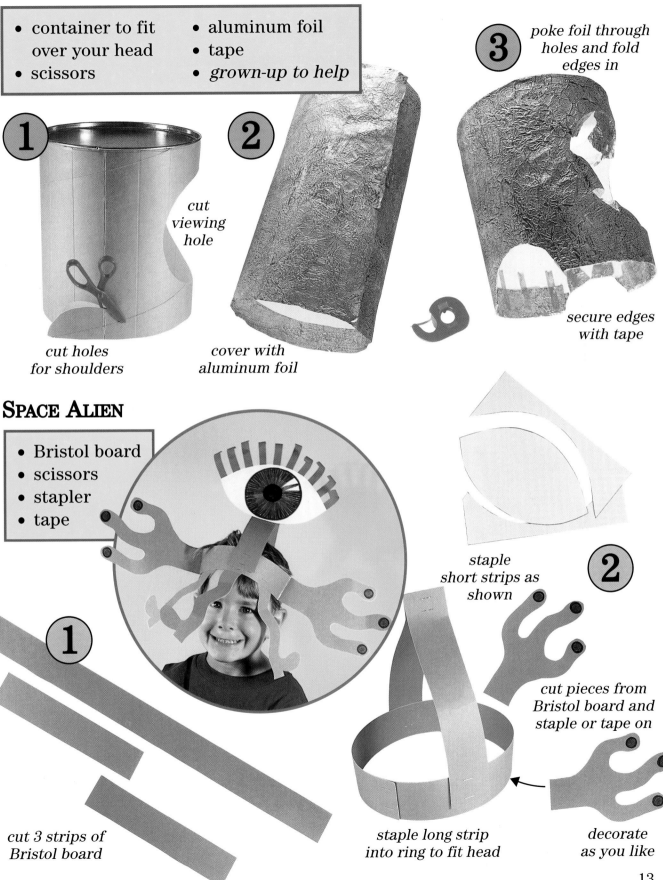

For carton like the one shown, ask at an ice cream parlor.
When stapling ring, see p. 5.

13

FACE PAINT FUN

- 1 spoonful of soft shortening
- 2 spoonfuls of corn starch
- bowl
- spoon
- ice-cube tray
- food coloring
- paintbrush
- warm water
- *grown-up to help*

① mix shortening and corn starch

② put some in one tray section for each color

③ add food coloring until you get the color you want

mix with spoon

blue + red = purple
blue + yellow = green
yellow + red = orange
yellow + red + blue = black

TIGER FACE

① be careful near eyes

dip finger in warm water, then in face paint

for details use a paintbrush dipped in warm water

② paint orange and white with your finger

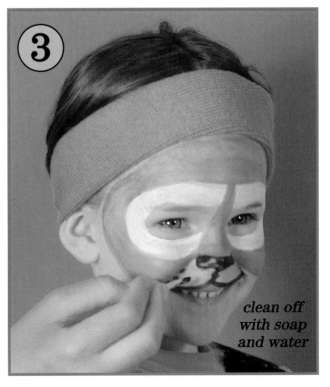

③ clean off with soap and water

add black details with paintbrush

For tiger costume, see p. 19.

DRESS-UP ZOO

REINDEER

- Bristol board
- stapler
- pencil
- paper
- scissors

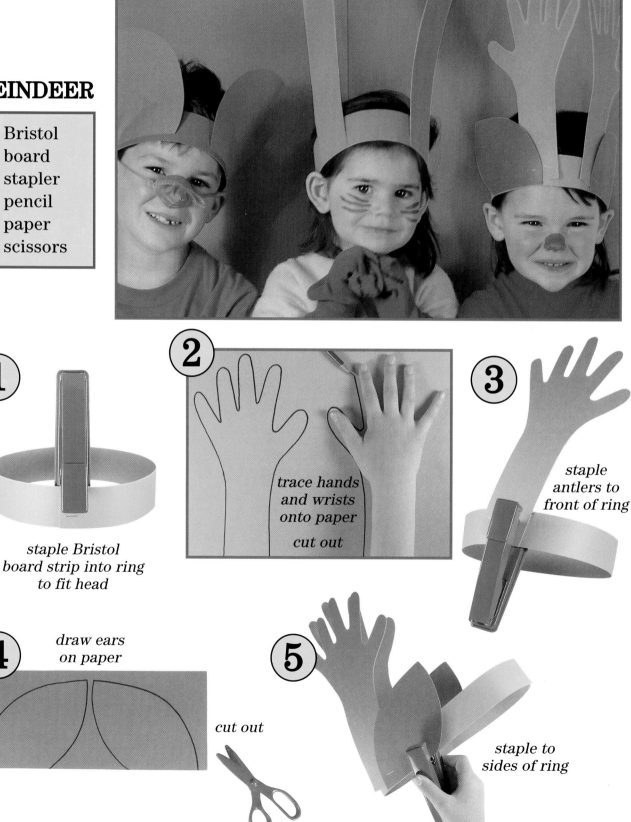

1 staple Bristol board strip into ring to fit head

2 trace hands and wrists onto paper
cut out

3 staple antlers to front of ring

4 draw ears on paper
cut out

5 staple to sides of ring

16

MOUSE

- Bristol board
- stapler
- pencil
- paper
- scissors
- clear tape
- hole punch
- yarn
- rope
- large safety pin

EARS

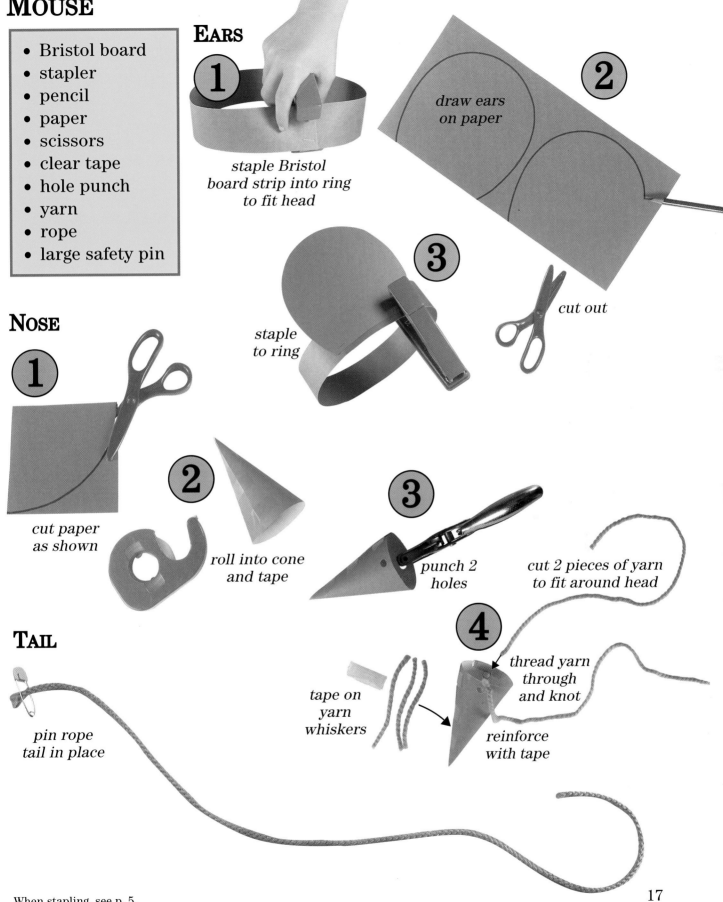

1 staple Bristol board strip into ring to fit head

2 draw ears on paper

3 staple to ring / cut out

NOSE

1 cut paper as shown

2 roll into cone and tape

3 punch 2 holes / cut 2 pieces of yarn to fit around head

4 tape on yarn whiskers / thread yarn through and knot / reinforce with tape

TAIL

pin rope tail in place

When stapling, see p. 5.

RABBIT

- Bristol board
- stapler
- pencil
- scissors
- 3 plastic bags
- twist tie
- large safety pin
- socks
- fabric paint

EARS

1 staple Bristol board strip into ring to fit head

2 draw ears on Bristol board

cut out

3 staple ears to ring

TAIL

1 cut tops and bottoms off bags

2 pile them on top of each other

3 gather as shown

4 twist in middle and fasten with twist tie

fluff tail and pin in place

PAWS

paint paw details on socks

slip socks onto hands

18

When stapling, see p. 5.

TIGER

- Bristol board
- pencil
- scissors
- stapler
- hole punch
- yarn
- stocking
- polyester stuffing
- large safety pin
- old sweatsuit
- acrylic paint and brush
- newspapers
- *grown-up to help*

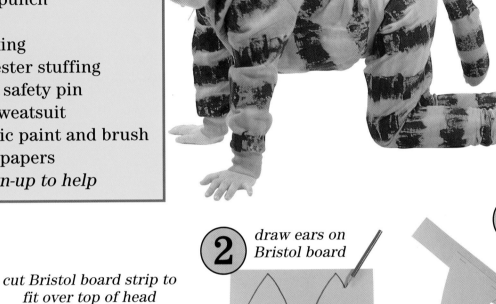

EARS

1 cut Bristol board strip to fit over top of head

2 draw ears on Bristol board

cut out

3 staple

4 punch 2 holes

fold up ears

thread yarn through and knot

TAIL

stuff tail and pin in place

SUIT

paint stripes on tail and sweatsuit

let dry before wearing

For face paint, see p. 14.

JOLLY JESTER

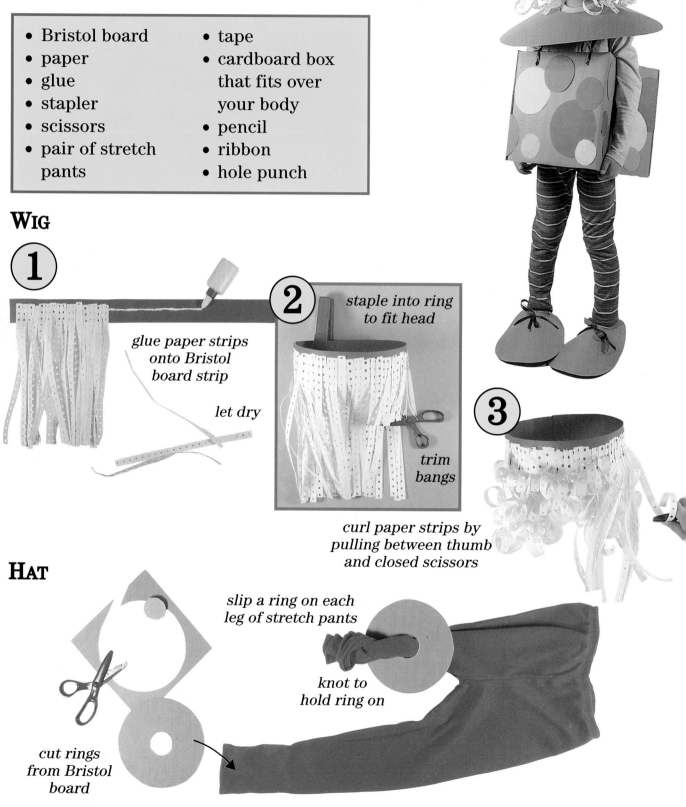

- Bristol board
- paper
- glue
- stapler
- scissors
- pair of stretch pants
- tape
- cardboard box that fits over your body
- pencil
- ribbon
- hole punch

WIG

1 glue paper strips onto Bristol board strip

let dry

2 staple into ring to fit head

trim bangs

3 curl paper strips by pulling between thumb and closed scissors

HAT

cut rings from Bristol board

slip a ring on each leg of stretch pants

knot to hold ring on

20

For face paint, see p. 14.
When stapling ring, see p. 5.

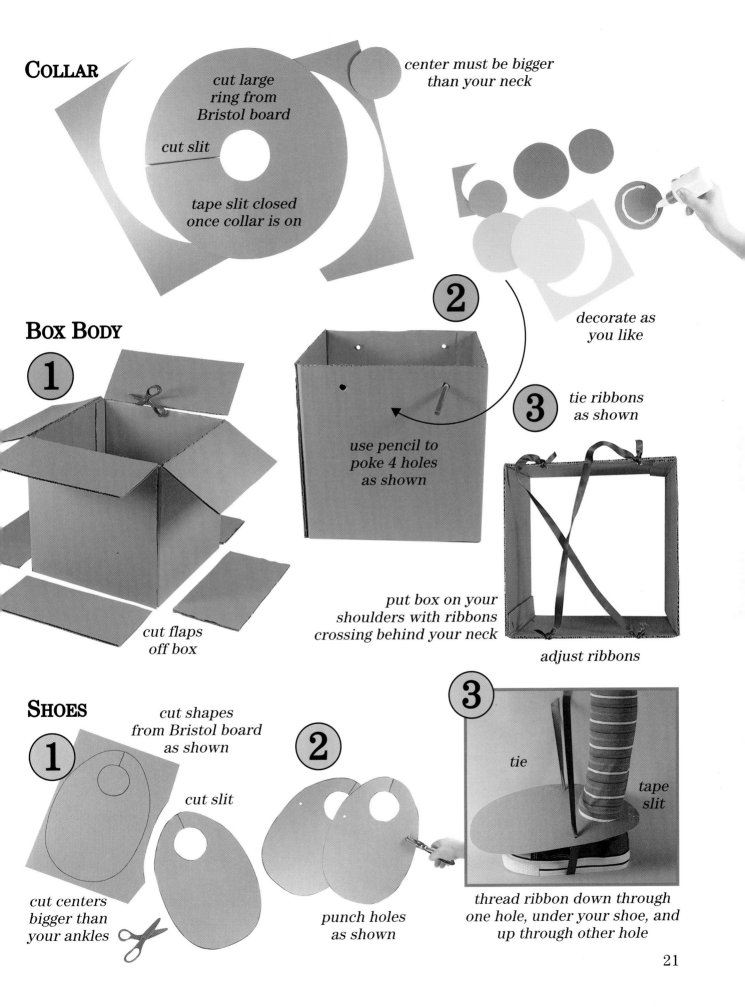

Collar

cut large ring from Bristol board

center must be bigger than your neck

cut slit

tape slit closed once collar is on

decorate as you like

Box Body

1

cut flaps off box

2

use pencil to poke 4 holes as shown

3

tie ribbons as shown

put box on your shoulders with ribbons crossing behind your neck

adjust ribbons

Shoes

1

cut shapes from Bristol board as shown

cut slit

cut centers bigger than your ankles

2

punch holes as shown

3

tie

tape slit

thread ribbon down through one hole, under your shoe, and up through other hole

ROBIN HOOD

- an old, large, long-sleeved T-shirt
- chalk
- scissors
- pencil
- paper
- safety pins
- corrugated cardboard
- hole punch
- rubber band
- *grown-up to help*

TUNIC

①

hat

belt

strap

tunic

pouch

use chalk to draw pieces on T-shirt

cut along chalk lines and use pieces as shown

HAT

1 use hat piece

2 roll up bottom

3 draw feather on paper — cut out

4 pin onto hat

BELT

1 cardboard — draw buckle shape

2 cut out — punch 4 holes

3 cut slits

thread belt piece through slits

4

5 fold straight end back and pin

run pointed end through and pull snug

6

POUCH

1 use pouch piece and snip 6 holes — cut fringe

2 thread strap piece in and out of holes — gather above fringe with rubber band

3 pull to close — knot

TOGA PARTY

GRECIAN ROBE

- 2 large pieces of fabric
- scissors
- ribbon

① fold a piece of fabric in half

cut slit for neck

② tie one piece of ribbon at waist

③ drape fabric on head and tie ribbon around it

tie sleeves up with ribbon

criss-cross a piece of ribbon across chest as shown and tie at back

For jewellery, see p. 6.

ROMAN TUNIC

- bath towel
- piece of rope

2

place over shoulder

1

fold towel in half

tie rope around waist

SANDALS

- corrugated cardboard
- pencil
- scissors
- hole punch
- 2 long ribbons

2

cut out

3

thread ribbon as shown

1

trace your feet on cardboard

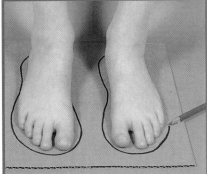

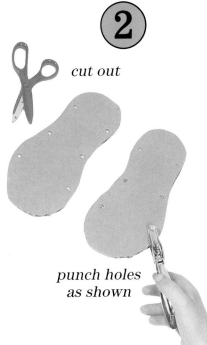

punch holes as shown

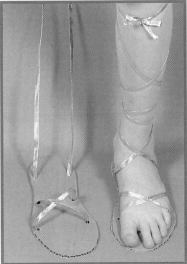

put feet in sandals and lace up around legs

MAGIC MAKER

- large piece of fabric
- ribbon
- pencil
- Bristol board
- scissors
- self-adhesive vinyl
- paint stir stick
- tape
- ribbons

ROBE

fold fabric
in half

cut slit
for neck

tie one piece of
ribbon at waist

decorate
with vinyl stars

STARS

1

draw circle
on Bristol
board

mark 5 dots as
shown

connect dots
to make star

cut out

2

cut out stars
and peel off
backing

trace pattern onto
self-adhesive vinyl

HAT

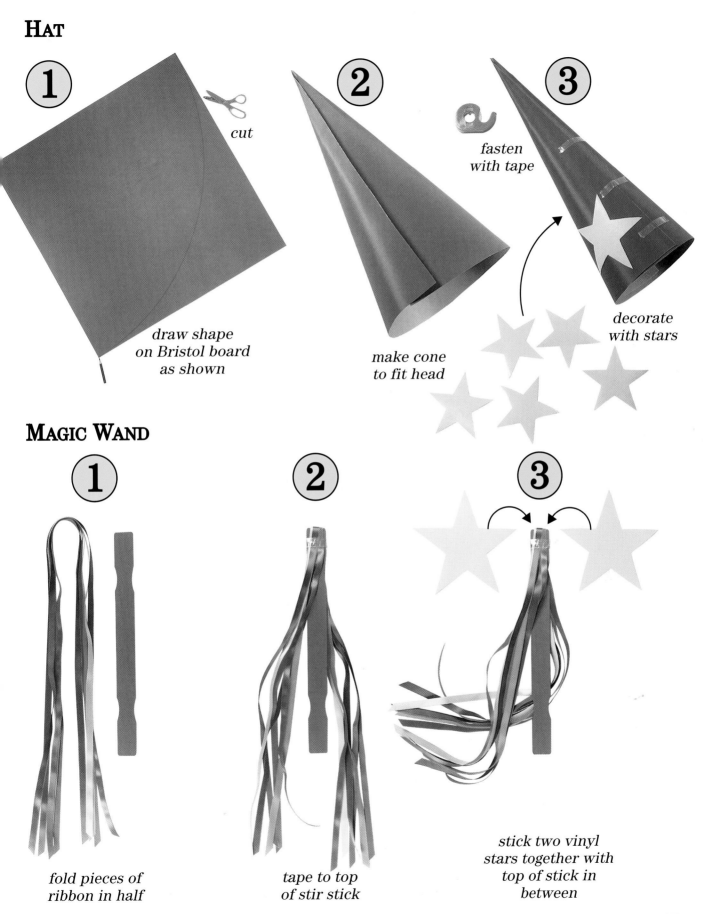

1 cut
draw shape
on Bristol board
as shown

2 make cone
to fit head

3 fasten
with tape
decorate
with stars

MAGIC WAND

1 fold pieces of
ribbon in half

2 tape to top
of stir stick

3 stick two vinyl
stars together with
top of stick in
between

FIT FOR ROYALTY

- tracing paper
- pencil
- scissors
- Bristol board
- stapler
- polyester stuffing
- glue
- paper tube
- *decorate as you like*

pattern

28

For cape, see p. 8.

CROWN

1

tracing paper

trace pattern and cut out

2

trace outline onto Bristol board 4 times as shown and cut out

3

staple into circle to fit head

4

overlap 2 opposite tall strips and staple flat as shown

5

match tips of other 2 tall strips and staple upright as shown

6

glue

decorate crown and cape

stuffing

glue

SCEPTER

measure tube and make a mini crown to fit

glue

When stapling ring, see p. 5.

ENCHANTED CASTLE

- 3 cardboard
  appliance boxes
- Bristol board
- scissors
- tape
- glue
- paper
- 2 drinking straws
- pencil
- rope
- tempera paint
- paintbrush
- *grown-up to help*
- *decorate as you like*

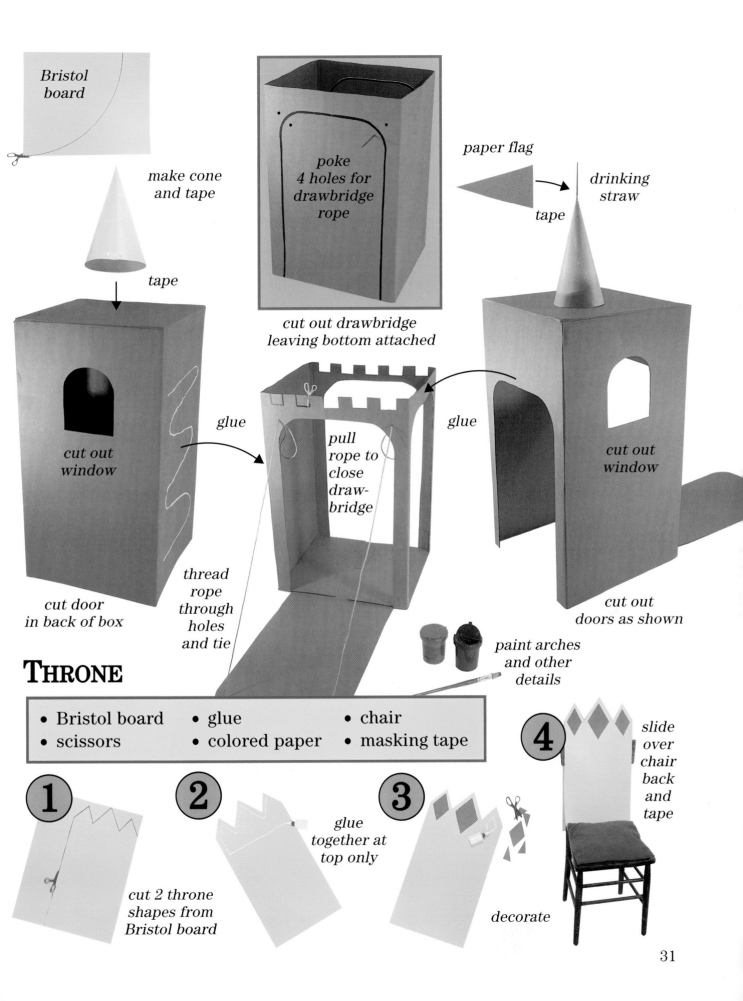

Bristol board

make cone and tape

tape

poke 4 holes for drawbridge rope

cut out drawbridge leaving bottom attached

paper flag

tape

drinking straw

cut out window

cut door in back of box

glue

thread rope through holes and tie

pull rope to close draw-bridge

glue

cut out window

cut out doors as shown

paint arches and other details

THRONE

• Bristol board	• glue	• chair
• scissors	• colored paper	• masking tape

1 cut 2 throne shapes from Bristol board

2 glue together at top only

3 decorate

4 slide over chair back and tape